Your Life Matters

Free Yourself from the Spiritual Junk
Choking Your Life

By

Catherine Lord

Thank you to Kat Kerr for teaching the soul doctor prayer through Elijah Streams, and for all the hope she has shared with the world. Thank you to Steve Shultz of Elijah List Ministries and Elijah Streams for making it all happen so people who desire true freedom can find it.

CONTENTS

HOW ARE THINGS WITH YOU?

Is there anyone to ask you that question? I know there have been times in my life when there was no one asking me that. There's lots of reasons for that and sometimes I was being too needy. But it can still be very lonely.

Are you lost? Or lonely? Are you struggling with business or about to lose your job? Maybe you live in a dying community and you don't see any future. Maybe you just feel so incredibly alone and forgotten.

So many stories have come my way lately about people who were totally forgotten by everyone and led lives of indescribable chaos. I feel such pain for these people. One recent story is of a man who was locked in a bedroom for twenty years. He finally had to set the house on fire so that the firefighters would rescue him. That news story has haunted me because there was no one to inquire after him. Even his extended family weren't really curious about him. How forgotten he must have felt. How brave of him to do what he did to get free. Why did never try to escape or set fire to the house years earlier? He was trapped and felt he had no chance.

Then there was the story by a woman who told of being treated like utter garbage by her family growing up because she was a girl and her birth culture doesn't have any value for girls. Her destiny was to be treated like garbage by her family until she could be sold in an arranged marriage. Her father abused her sexually and allowed his friends to abuse her. She went to school and was surrounded by adults and authorities but somehow her somewhat ragged condition and the problems she presented were never inquired into by anyone. Her family would beat her and lock her in her room. She was never free to speak to people outside her home.

When she finally escaped her family she immediately got tangled up with a man who was a user and abuser. However, he seemed to care about her and being with him meant she was free of needing her family's financial support, so, she stayed with him, for years. She had his children and was his wife but he always treated her like garbage.

Unlike the man in the closet, she lived on the outside world and she ran successful businesses. Her husband didn't work so all the money coming in was hers. One would think she would realize that it was always in her power to leave him and establish herself successfully without him, yet she never could see that. All she could see were the invisible bars keeping her trapped in the life. It was her son who finally forced her to take a risk and leave. She had never known freedom, never had anyone care about her. She was still stuck on the idea that being with this man had freed her from her family. She eventually saw that it wasn't freedom but a trap. However, nothing in her life had ever prepared her for freedom and she couldn't see what to do. It was the love of her grown son that finally opened her eyes to the pain she was inflicting on herself. He gave her the courage to leave to seek a better life.

The story that has haunted me the most has been the one I've followed for years now about the hundreds of girls who were used and abused by so-called grooming gangs. The girls were described as coming from trashy families where the parents were drug or alcohol abusers or worse. The girls were basically throwaway people. Whether they were trashy or not they got labeled as trashy and that made them people no one cared about. The authorities didn't care, and it was their job is to enforce the current laws that would have prevented or stopped the abuse. No one cared about them, so therefore no one cared when they were being abused. Only by naming and shaming have some of the authorities finally been forced to care.

Up to now, the rights of the groomers were considered more important than the lives of these girls from poor backgrounds. The description of what happened to them was that, as girls from abusive or drug-addicted families, they were frequently without food, or basic necessities, or without anyone to show love to them. Then, along came these men who offered presents and affection, and it seemed like heaven. They lived the dream for a short bit – until they discovered they were being set up to be prostitutes. I imagine some of those girls never believed the truth and accepted the prostitution as the price of the "love" being offered them. Others probably realized that they had been duped but couldn't see a way out so they stayed in the life and adapted to protect what was left of their souls.

Once again, something that had been presented to them as freedom turned out to be enslavement, while true freedom was beyond their ability to grasp.

My heart just aches for these people. How many people have I walked past in my life who I thought were weird or were being difficult and they were actually leading horrible lives just out of sight of everyone around them and yet still in plain view of all? The man who was locked up for twenty years in the bedroom, all his neighbors and former classmates and their families are left wondering how they could have not noticed that after about the age of twelve no one ever saw him in public again. Everyone in that community is asking themselves how all their civil society mass-failed when it came to this young man. His classmates asked about him but a welfare check produced satisfactory answers from the parents and so he was forgotten. No one asked about him, no one missed him, no one saw anything weird in the behavior of his father and stepmother, no one ever wondered what happened to him. He just disappeared into a bedroom and no help ever came until the day he decided to take his fate into his own hands.

Do any of these scenarios sound like you? Have terrible things happened to you and it seemed like no one noticed? No one came? The cavalry never showed up?

Maybe your life hasn't been quite as dramatically bad as what I've described but you've had difficult struggles that you thought you would never survive. Maybe you got cancer, or your parents died when you were young, or, like me, someone moved in on your life and just took sort of took you over. You thought that person loved you so you let them do it. You thought by being with them you were experiencing freedom but it turned out to be a lie and a trap. When your family or friends opposed your choice, you gave up your family and friends because your captor convinced you that your family was jealous and that life in captivity was actually freedom for you.

When you finally realized the trap, you were in a bad spot. Now what do you do? You staked it all on this one gamble, and you lost. Now your life is a wreck. How do you recover? Once you get out of the situation, how do you swallow your pride and all the "I told you so's" and go back to estranged family and former friends? Maybe in the meantime you now have children and so you are forever tied to that person no matter how desperately you wish to be free.

Do you feel trapped in your life? Does it feel sometimes like the walls are closing in on you? Or is it that you feel empty?

Maybe it goes a totally different way for you – maybe you have a good life or even a great life, but the inside of your life is based on nothing solid even though it looks solid. There is nothing meaningful to hold it together. You yourself are hollow and it aches. You push the hollowness away and you tell yourself that you are living your dream, but there are times in the night when you know deep down it's not true. Your spouse looks to the outside world like a loving spouse, your children appear to be excellent creatures, you look successful in your work, but things are wrong behind the scenes. As one of my friends said, "I wish I led the life everyone on Facebook thinks I lead."

Our society right now is pushing people harder than has happened in a long time to give up all the core bedrock principles that make our lives worth having. We're being told that any sense of higher purpose is silly, that morality is an enslavement to something. People who have questions about themselves and their identities are being encouraged to embrace the confusion under the idea that the confusion will bring them freedom. But once again, that sort of confusion and chaos is a deception and people who embrace the chaos don't find freedom, they find pain and enslavement. The deception can be so complete, however, that some of them aren't able to see it for what it is until it is almost too late. Some never do see it.

We're being pushed to think that we can have our own truth and that "our truth" doesn't have to match anyone else's truth. But here's a question to ponder – why do the same people who say there is no standard of truth for anything also insist you adhere to building codes? Think about that one for a minute. County, state, and local authorities everywhere insist that you have to have proper lighting and proper plumbing that follows a strict set of rules and there is no leeway at all for "your truth" when it comes to passing an inspection. There is the proper way and that's it. However, for all the decisions that can destroy you personally and leave you forever in torment, the same people might tell you to just wing it. Some of the decisions they want you to wing it on is the stuff that can ruin your life. The "your truth" kind of thinking is a trap being sold to you as freedom.

We have become a society that hassles people forever on all the little stuff like building codes and speech codes while at the same time we fill each other's lives with muck and garbage and pretend we like the results.

Maybe you have devoted your life to a cause, or to several causes. Some causes are righteous but even the righteous ones can get taken over by people with bad agendas. Some causes are being sold to you as freedom and salvation for the world but they are actually a trap. The solutions offered by the leaders of the cause have more to do with making rules and forcing people to give money and almost nothing to do with fixing the problems the cause is highlighting. Their "solutions" to bring freedom just mean perpetual enslavement to ever-expanding rules and taxes.

Maybe you actually joined up with a cause, not because you cared about it but because it was a way to get power. You enjoyed the power and the sense of confidence and authority it gave you. But that kind of power can be corrupted easily and you may find now that, once again, the "freedom" to wield power over others has turned out to be a trap for you. The people you wielded power over have long resented it and the first chance they get to get rid of you, they'll take it. Your "freedom" landed you in a bad place.

Many times people find that causes they passionately believed in are being led by people who are actually working to maintain the very things their cause is fighting against. Those leaders are sometimes even using all the donations to line their own pockets. They spend far more time keeping the true-believers in line and sending out appeals for more money than they do going after the people they were supposed to be opposing. It can be heart-breaking to realize that you have been used so badly. If the cause itself is corrupted on top of that then you have been hit with a double betrayal.

The power of evil is always seeking to trap people. The power of evil can take over any agenda where people are not wary and it can corrupt people around you who started out with good intentions. The first crime ever was written about in the Bible. Traps and deceits are nothing new. What seems "new" about it is that it's happening to you.

Don't give up. Please don't give up.

There is help to be had but sometimes the noise in our lives, or worse, the noise in our heads, is so loud it stops us from hearing the solutions. It blocks us from hearing God. God planned an identity for you. God planned a beautiful and successful life for you. The things offered by this world that are put to you as "freedom" are a deception – they enslave you, they strip your soul, they leave you hollow and empty. You get eaten up inside and sometimes then your body starts eating itself up, too, as it lives out the chaos or the emptiness inside your spirit.

It can seem like the solutions out there don't really help. The last hundred years or more we've all been told that mental health and emotional health are the main thing, and the only thing, and that they outrank even morality. It's far more important for you to have proper mental health or emotional health, "your truth," than it is for you to do good in this world or to treat others right. That's what we're told. We're also told that any of several forms of "counseling" will help. And, to be fair, sometimes it does.

I went through years of therapy with different counselors. They managed to help me with some things but some of the truths they pointed out, it seemed like I could hear it and understand it but when I tried to apply their suggestions it didn't seem to work somehow. The place they were trying to help me get to seemed a long way off. It was like they were trying to tell me important things but I was so far away it didn't seem to have any reality in my life, and most of them had no way to bridge the gap. They could throw out advice but they were powerless to reach me. Very few of them had anything truly solid for me to even stand on because they didn't believe in anything beyond themselves. In time, what these counselors tried to help me learn was swept away by the next big crisis. Try as I might, I couldn't make a breakthrough so I could get better. I could almost see where I needed to be, but I felt powerless to get there.

The issues that took me to a counselor all had strong spiritual aspects. Counselors mostly approach things strictly from mental health or emotional health. I tried to divorce all the different parts of me and just stick to mental health or emotional health but it didn't work. All these pieces of ourselves are interwoven and it isn't right or healthy to try to split things off from each other. They wanted to deal only with one part of me, as though you could compartmentalize yourself and shut away the other parts to deal with one thing only.

I would be willing to bet that what most of us need to talk about involves spiritual pain.

After years of being used up by other people, and making bad choices, and getting involved in causes and situations and with people who I felt used me and left me, I felt empty inside. I was desperate to fill the emptiness and I tried a lot of things that were really bad for me. That was my trouble, I had already compartmentalized my experiences away from the other parts of me so I could stop being in pain. Going to a counselor to do more of the same wasn't helpful, but that's what we're told to do, and we're told it will help, so I went, and I tried.

I had some good counselors and they meant well. But I didn't walk away with lasting change and I paid a lot of money to not get better. There has to be a better way.

Maybe you tried psychiatry, or psychology, or a self-help book, or a fitness program, or a diet. Maybe you tried the church and you got hurt, or you still felt empty. Nothing has worked. You went to sessions, you bought books, you hunted up friends, you tried yoga, you tried all the latest mental health fads – primal scream, anyone? Some of you have literally tried almost anything in order to get help. There is help. Don't give up. Keep reading.

Is it Possible to be Wounded in Your Soul?

Is it possible to be broken inside you in your mind, body or spirit and to feel broken? Yes, it is. Is it possible that these wounds could create physical illnesses? Yes, it is. A soul wound is when something inside of you is broken and it's affecting every other part of your life. You feel lost. You maybe don't know what is wrong, you just know that you are desperate to find answers you can't find.

It manifests in the damage you are doing to your life that is making you crazy. You keep going around doing stupid things that harm yourself. You sabotage yourself in your career, in your marriage, with your family, or in your other relationships. You get involved in drugs or alcohol and now you have even more problems. You hook up with wildly impossible people and then pretend you're happy. You do stupid things to your body and pretend that you're happy.

Maybe you got involved with porn and now you have tracking software on your computer and the porn didn't satisfy. Maybe you let total strangers online impress you into giving them big sums of money, or you allowed others to love bomb you into making completely life-transformational changes to yourself. And you did these things because you were lost and lonely and you believed you were going to be loved by them forever if you did it. Then, if the transformations were too much, the people who had love-bombed you into it now are angry with you for having doubts and they abandon you.

Maybe you went and gambled to get some money to solve your problems. Except it never works that way so you gambled a little more, and then you gambled your paycheck, and then you gambled the money you borrowed from work, and then the money you borrowed to pay your bills, only you didn't use it to pay your bills. And now you're in so deep on the losses and the gambling that you could be in serious trouble.

Are you drinking or drugging to cover the emptiness inside? Or eating too much? Or addicted to cosmetology?

Maybe something happened to you in the past that completely broke you and you've never been able to get better since then. Maybe you did something for which you feel you can never be forgiven. Or, you went through a trauma that no one else knows about. You don't know how to fix it, you don't even know how to tell people, so you just get in this perpetual cycle of hiding it and hiding everything about yourself in order to keep the secret.

Sometimes you just want to give up because you think you are beyond help. Sometimes it gets to the point where you want to just walk away and never come back and let people think you're dead rather than know the truth. Sometimes we think actual death will solve it.

The belief that you can't be fixed or that you can't be healed is a lie from the pit of hell and that mis-belief is what we're going to tackle right now. Believing you are so far gone as to be unreachable is a lie that keeps you stuck. If the power of evil can tie you up to the point where you lose all effectiveness, then evil wins. So, ditch that. You can be healed and you can and will be forgiven. You can be fixed and we're going to start that process right now.

Your life matters.

You can be saved.

Hang on to that. You CAN be saved.

So what's the source of your problems?

What you may not know is that you are loaded up with spiritual gunk, and slime, and old wounds, and clutter, and it's holding you back. It's holding you back to where you probably can't hear or see any of the good things happening in your life and you can't see any future for yourself. It can literally blind and deafen you and cloud your understanding.

If someone stopped you in the street this very minute and told you everything you needed to know in five easy sound bites, would you even hear them? Or would you stand there thinking, "Yeah, right, easy for YOU to say." Or even, "Who ARE you?" Or, would you be mildly interested, but still remain profoundly convinced that your problems are beyond help? There's people everywhere with books and social media of all sorts doing this very thing – they tell you what's wrong and share with you what they believe will fix your problems. People buy their books or listen to their videos and still don't get helped. The advice could be the best advice in the world but somehow it isn't reaching you. If you even retain it, it isn't reaching you deeply enough to help you in a lasting way.

Are you convinced that your problems are just so much worse than anyone else's and no one in the world has ever had it as bad as you? If you are then that is a sign that your life is so filled with spiritual junk it is keeping everything good out of your life. Our job is to get all the spiritual junk off you and out of your life. Cleanse you of spiritual slime, allow the light into your life to heal spiritual wounds. Once it's gone, your eyes, your ears and your understanding will all be opened.

THERE IS HEALING

I'm here to tell you that you can get free, and it won't take years.

So, how do we do that? It's the simplest of all prayers and it works in minutes. How it works depends on how you process things and how much spiritual clutter there is in your life.

For some of us, we just need to start with the prayer and pray it because we work through things by being busy. We don't want to take a lot of time out of life. We have a lot to do and we need to keep moving. Some of my best meditation times come when I'm driving or when I'm doing housework. My busy left brain is occupied which frees my right brain to listen to God and to flow creatively.

Some people need to talk it out in a group setting, or to a counselor, or confess to a minister or priest, while others need to be by themselves and have some quiet time.

Other people need to write it out. They don't see what God is saying to them until they put it on paper. Something about the writing process helps them work through the issue and see things they didn't see before. Others need to draw it out. By creating pictures or artwork of some type, they find a vent to express what they can't put into words.

Everybody has their own way. If you don't know what way works for you, then this book offers you several possibilities. This book sets out to help you by providing a format that will allow you as much flexibility as possible to process your baggage so you can get rid of it.

PRELIMINARY NOTE

There is one thing it is really important for you to understand – you were created by God, to be exactly the person you are, to use exactly the gifts God gave you. Stop rolling your eyes. Isn't that why you are here, to get rid of the junk and find out who you really are?

So, what happened along the way from that beautiful baby you started out as, to the messed up person you are right now?

Well, life is what happened.

Over time we all get gunked up by things that happened to us – bad decisions, betrayals, missed opportunities, traumatic events, you name it. And it all leaves behind spiritual junk.

We make bad choices and get into all kinds of garbage we shouldn't be into. We read stuff that leaves behind bits of evil clinging to us like slime. We go to movies we shouldn't have gone to, we make friends with people who are bad for us, we marry people who bring out all our worst tendencies, we worry about money so we betray someone in order to secure our own position. It happens. And then we get so full of spiritual slime and bad feelings that we get to where we can't function.

People at church try to help, but most church people are just ordinary people and they don't have superman communication skills. They are just themselves. They want to help so they try to give comfort or offer advice. They do whatever they hope will help. Maybe they phrase things awkwardly or they use cliches. And then there's us, standing there, all full of our own pain, and all we hear are the cliches or the awkwardness and we don't hear the kind intentions behind the words. So, we roll our eyes or even get offended with them. Now the church person is suffering a wound and they sometimes walk away feeling like no good deed will go unpunished. And the cycle repeats.

Or maybe the church person really did have good things to say and phrased it all beautifully, but we were so full of spiritual junk that we couldn't appreciate anything they were trying to do.

Maybe you don't trust church so you wouldn't have listened no matter what was said, good, bad, or indifferent.

Which one are you? Are you the one who refuses to be comforted, or the one who wants to be comforted but can't seem to hear or retain anything anyone says? Or, are you the one who wouldn't believe anyone no matter what?

AND WHAT ABOUT GOD?

God is trying to reach us. He's trying to help us, He's there for us, He never leaves us. But we're so full of junk we can't see anything He does and we can't hear His voice. We get to where we think we have no choices in life. We don't understand the freedom God gives us. We laugh bitterly at the idea that we still have freedom. We don't see that we have the power to make any choices at all. We don't understand anything.

FORGIVENESS

A huge part of the prayer is forgiveness. Forgiving the people who caused the bad things that happened to you, or that you feel didn't do enough to stop the bad things, or who set out to deliberately harm you. There are also some people who genuinely never did anything to harm you but you believe they did and you've carried that bitterness for a long time.

I know you don't want to forgive some of these people. You're probably saying to yourself, "But they did really bad things to me! I can't just let all that go! They've never once asked to be forgiven so why should I let them off the hook?!"

I get it. I do. I couldn't say it, either, about certain people, not at first. But let me put this to you a different way.

I'm not asking you to just nonchalantly let serious things go as though they don't matter. I've been through some bad stuff myself. I had to learn this prayer, too. I'm telling you that this prayer works.

This prayer is about saving your life. Even if the people never ask you for forgiveness, when you forgive them you get poison out of your soul that is eating you up inside. Don't believe me? Let's take a look at the things that happen to people who carry bitterness and hate and misery around with them.

I know someone who adored her father and he adored her. But something went badly wrong in his life and when she was a teenager, her beloved father committed suicide. She was the one who found his body. She went many years with that hanging over her and it affected her and her whole life and her children. She was an alcoholic throughout her children's growing up years and left them with some tough memories to get over. Her father's suicide hung over her like a pall and the fallout affects even her grandchildren. Way down underneath she blamed herself for his suicide for years.

I've known people who went crazy over a girlfriend or boyfriend leaving them and they tried to shoot up the apartment house at night or stalk their ex or do terrible things to them. One guy I know went and pitched a huge scene in front of his soon-to-be ex-wife's house in the middle of the night and roused all the neighbors while he was at it. He was stinking drunk and he got arrested and went to jail. After that he had trouble getting jobs. He had to start a new career late in life and had to get people to trust him again. Like it or not, his wife had a right to leave and throwing such a fit about it didn't make her want to come back. In the end, him making such a scene just caused himself a lot of trouble without making his life one bit better.

People get involved with drugs or some other addiction and some of them steal money from everyone they know. They tell lies, they scheme, they manipulate so that they can keep their addiction going. Nobody is important enough for them to treat that person fairly if that person is coming between them and their addiction. They destroy their families and friendships with their stupid games to get another fix.

On top of that, they have an exaggerated sense of themselves and they spend their lives believing people are out to get them or that people go out of their way to hurt them. They drive everyone around them crazy with all their manipulations and their neediness.

People have lost someone in an accident and it just tears them apart inside until they were so full of rage and pain they want to destroy everything and everyone around them. And often they do just that.

People get passed over for something they felt they were owed and then spend their lives trying to subtly destroy everyone around them to get revenge, or, plotting ways to steal back what they felt they were owed. They become so full of poison that no one wants to be around them and they destroy any good feelings anyone ever had about them. All their friends and family want to do is get away from them. If the person successfully gets what they feel is proper revenge, well, then they won. But now they have far fewer friends and nothing to show for their life but pain and hatred. So, what exactly did they win?

Is this who you want to be? You shake your head over these types of stories but what if you are becoming like those nasty, angry people? What if you've already been harming the people around you with the toxicity you're carrying with you? I don't think you want that.

I don't think you want to be the person who is so eaten up with rage or jealousy or greed or fear that everyone you know starts to shun you. Maybe you already are that person and people are already shunning you. For some people, knowing they are out of control and that people are shunning them just makes them harder to deal with.

Maybe you've seen the look in your spouse's eyes when you've done something so incredibly foul to them that even YOU know it was bad. You can't stand seeing the fear and loathing you've created in them staring back at you. So, what do you do but try to force that fear and loathing look away by getting nastier. Then the look gets replaced with a dead look. Is that somehow better?

Maybe you don't vent toxicity on others, maybe you turn it in on yourself.

Are you the person who has been so hurt by others that you no longer trust and you no longer commit to anything? Eventually people see that you have great gifts but they will learn if they haven't already they can't count on you for anything so they quit asking. Well, you got what you wanted, people don't bother you anymore, but is that really want you wanted?

Maybe you oversleep your job interviews, or show up late and do poorly. You start turning in sloppy work at work, or you're difficult and nasty to deal with. You berate your coworkers or your employees. You're sarcastic and bitter. Or you just don't communicate at all.

Maybe as a boss you have favorites and scapegoats and you like the idea that people jump in fear when you come around and rush to suck up to you so you won't make them your scapegoat.

Maybe you shy away from anything that would make you successful. You're clearly good at something and you have all these people begging you to just do what you're good at it because it would solve problems for them, too. You embrace it for awhile and make plans, but then you start screwing up or start falling apart. Maybe you're one of the ones who lecture people to leave you alone and shame them into it with a big display of your need for privacy. Wow. And you think this will make you happy.

Maybe you have been choosing the worst people for friends and lovers, and you do it over and over again. How are you managing to pick person after person to be around who is so terrible for you? It may not be your fault because of things that warped you in previous experiences, but continuing in this path is completely self-destructive. Eventually, it becomes true that YOU are destroying you. Why? Why would you do that?

In some of these scenarios, you become a self-fulfilling prophecy. But who prophesied failure over you and why would you want that? Get rid of it! You don't have to accept those words! You don't have to talk to yourself that way, either! You don't have to be the kind of person who can never succeed because you constantly sabotage yourself. There is a better way!

I'm not the only one who has said these things to you. I bet there are other people who have probably tried to tell you not to destroy yourself. But you're the only one who can make the choice. Do you want to be better? If emptiness and jealousy and rage are what you want then you have it.

You're holding in your hands a book that will help you. This prayer can help you be better, but you have to choose it.

I think, from the fact that you picked up this book, means you want to run away from what you've become or what you see yourself becoming. You just don't know how.

Well, here's how.

The way you have been handling past trauma is NOT serving you. So, stop being too proud to accept help. Stop being so arrogant as to think that no one else has ever been through what you're going through. They have. Lots of people have been through terrible traumas, you're not the only one. There IS help for you but you have to choose to accept the help.

I want you to think for a minute about the worst things in your life that ever happened to you. Why would you want to keep that stuff? It's horrible! You have the power to get rid of all that spiritual pain. Take it and do it!

Father God never wanted you to be so filled with pain that you can't function. You are His precious child. Together we're going to help you release it so that you can find the sweetness He has for you. But it involves forgiveness and a choice you have to make to save yourself from the pain. You're going to have to forgive people. If they deserve earthly justice, fine, but you need to come at it from a place where you are seeking justice and not revenge. People will see the revenge element and turn away but they will be drawn to a cause of justice.

PERSONAL POWER

You do have choices. They may be small ones but you do have them. However, this book is not about how to make good choices. It's about freeing you from the junk so that you can see that you still have choices and where you should turn for clarity.

STEP ONE

Your first step in this exercise is you get to make a choice. I'm going to ask you something and you need to decide if you will do it. If you think your life has stripped you of all your choices, you do still have at least one choice left.

What I'm asking you to do is read this prayer, and I'm asking you to read it OUT LOUD.

That's it.

I want you to say the prayer out loud. I'm asking you to commit to your own reclamation enough to be willing to do that.

"That's it?" you ask incredulously.

"Yes, that's it," I answer you.

"Why?" you ask.

I want you to read it out loud because it changes something in the spirit. Reading it silently changes some things but saying it out loud changes things even more. I wish I could give you some really cool, deeply philosophical answer. I can just tell you that it changes things.

Maybe it's because by speaking it into the spiritual atmosphere, you make your intention clear. This is an act of your will, not of your emotions. Your emotions may tell you that this prayer hurts too much and that you can't do it or that you won't do it. So, it's going to be an act of your will to do it anyway. By speaking this act of your will out loud into the spiritual atmosphere, it changes things. It changes things in the spirit and it changes things in you.

Some of you are rolling your eyes over this explanation. So, I answer you – what does it matter how it works? If it works, it works. Later on, when you're all better and your life is vastly improved, you will have the time to work on the secrets of God's universe. Right now, we need to get you free so you can do all those wonderful things. So, let's do this.

Besides, what have you got to lose? I mean, really? You were so driven to find change that you picked up this book. Why not do what it says?

STEP TWO

You must read the ENTIRE prayer, both parts. There are things in it you won't want to say. Say it anyway. All I can tell you is it will change everything.

There you go, there are your two choices – 1) Choose to read it all, and, 2) Choose to read it out loud. You don't have to believe the words, you just have to say them. If you don't want to be heard by anyone else, that's okay with God. He prefers you to go to some private place to have your conversations with Him anyway. Go off by yourself and work this out.

I mentioned that there are two parts to the prayer. There's the part where you get rid of stuff, and then there's the part where you fill the newly emptied space with something good. You have to do both parts. If you leave the space empty, it will be too easy to fill it back up with all the same junk or worse. Do both parts of the prayer.

THE PRAYER

"As an act of my will, not because I want to but because I choose to, I release all the junk from my life. I release fear. I say it again. I release FEAR.

"I release rage, anxiety, tension, and misplaced anger.

"I release all jealousy, envy, and greed. I release all thoughts that other people have things I should have, that other people have things I bitterly resent them having. I release all desire to be angry or resentful over what other people have. I release all desire to be angry or resentful over what I think I don't have.

"I release all thoughts that I am poor. I release all desire to ever describe myself as 'poor' again. I release all thoughts of poverty and want. I release all thoughts that others have too much or that they have too little. I release all desire to make fun of people with money, and all desire to make fun of people with no money. I release all desire to make cutting remarks to people about money or lack of it. I release all desire to obsess over money, either the lack of it or the riches of it. I release all fear that I won't have enough or that I won't be able to pay my bills. If I have money, I release all sense of guilt over having the money and I release all need to "prove" things to people. I release all fear that even though I have money I might lose it and be poor again. I release all agendas that I have tied to money, either having it, or not having it.

"I release pain. I release all trauma, and I release all memories of the past that involve trauma. I release sadness and grief and sorrow. I release all sense of being abandoned. I release all memories of death and murder and suicide that may be in my past or my family's past. I release any trauma from previous generations that might have been passed on to me. I release all anger over the trauma, all sense of betrayal. All sense of loss. I release all desire to not forgive someone else for pain or trauma. I release all desire to not forgive myself. I release all depression, especially 'clinical' depression.

"I release betrayal. I release all the times someone has betrayed me and I release all times where I myself betrayed someone else. I release all pain from times when people have hurt me, and I release all pain from times when I have hurt others, intentionally or accidentally. Known and unknown.

"I release all generational pain. I release all the times when I think my family suffered something terrible or that my ancestors suffered something that I feel was unjust. I release all times that I may not know about when someone thought the same of my family or my ancestors. I release all desire to not forgive.

"I release all pain from someone in my family or among my friends who left me by committing suicide. I release all anger, pain, shattering loss, especially if I was the one who found their body, or someone I know was the one. I release all sense of betrayal at that person for having abandoned me. As an act of my will, I forgive them.

"I release all pain from times when I wanted to kill myself. I release the sadness, the grief, the despair I felt, and I forgive the people who didn't see or understand. I forgive the people I blamed at the time for making me feel so sad.

"I release all pain from any abortion I ever had, including any pain that's hidden because I may think I have no feelings about it. I release any guilt I have about it and I repent and ask God's forgiveness. I release all trauma from choices I may have felt were forced upon me, whether by my own choices or by pressure from others. As an act of my will I forgive myself and I forgive anyone involved in it. I give the child back to God and I release any anger or despair or other feelings about the people who performed the abortion or counseled me to get it. If I ever pushed someone to have an abortion, then to the best of my ability I nullify those words and I ask mercy for the person I pressured.

"As an act of my will, I release all pain from accidents that I suffered, or accidents I may have caused. As a first responder or as a medical person, I release all trauma from injuries I have witnessed, accidents I had to tend to, family drama and pain from other people that affected me from those situations.

"As a current member of the military or as former military, or as a member of law enforcement, I release all pain for anything that happened as an act of war that I participated in, or as an act of law enforcement. I release all pain for traumatic things I witnessed, for the suffering I witnessed, for pain and tragedy I had to be a part of.

"As an act of my will, I release all pain about acts of war that were done to me or my family or my people. I release all pain about acts of law enforcement that harmed me or anyone I know. I release all pain from acts of crime that harmed me while I was performing my duties. I let it go and as act of my will, I forgive everyone, including myself.

"I release all anger and shame and frustration over things that were done to me due to a policy by a government at any level. I release all desire to hurt people to get revenge. If I helped create a government policy that harmed people, I ask forgiveness and I forgive myself and the people I worked with who helped develop this policy.

"As an act of my will, I release any pain from any crimes done against me, and as an act of my will, I turn over to God and to

His earthly authorities any necessity to handle the punishment for that crime.

"As an act of my will, I repent of any crimes I have committed and I call back as much as is possible the words I spoke, the deeds I did, the lies I told, and I ask for mercy to those I harmed.

"As an act of my will, I release any pain from any incarceration to which I was remanded, justly or unjustly, at the hands of judges, lawyers, guards, law enforcement, fellow inmates, or society. As an act of my will I forgive everyone.

"As a spouse, I release all pain for acts of violence my spouse had to witness or that happened to them, or that they did to someone else. I release all pain of being the spouse and having to sit by and watch my spouse go through things that I couldn't prevent or stop.

"I release all pain I experienced having to be the spouse of someone who has gone through some bad stuff and maybe couldn't explain what was wrong. I release all pain for times when I found myself cast as the bad guy in the relationship when I'm just the spouse. I release all pain for the times when my spouse took their feelings out on me. I forgive my spouse for everything.

"As an act of my will, I release any pain from my father or my mother, my siblings, my spouse, my children, or my extended family. I release any pain from childhood trauma and I forgive myself for what I believed I did to deserve it. As an act of my will I forgive anyone who harmed me. If the words 'father' or 'mother' are painful to me then I release any anger I have ever had about those words. I release any pain from physical abuse, emotional abuse, or mental abuse. I renounce anything I was made to believe about deserving it and I give myself permission to leave the situation.

"As an act of my will, I renounce everything anyone has ever said to me that promised evil to my life, that hurt my feelings, that left me feeling valueless or unworthy. I release all memories of people who questioned my competence, who indicated I wasn't worthy of my salary, of people who dismissed me as unimportant. I release all those words and I release all pain associated with them. For any doom prophesied over my life, whether by people who meant to harm me, by medical people giving me a diagnosis, by family or friends labeling me as unimportant, or by anyone else, I refuse those words entry into my life. I nullify the words and I forgive the people who spoke them.

"As an act of my will, I renounce anything evil I ever participated in, knowingly or unknowingly, and I close any doors to evil that my participation opened into my life. I renounce bad language and the times when I have said filthy things to people, including insults and angry words. I nullify the power of any words I wish I had never spoken. I release all memories of times when angry, insulting things were said to me and I nullify the power of any filthy language that ever entered my life.

"I renounce any attachment to alcohol and to illegal use of drugs, including prescription drugs. I renounce any attachments to gambling, porn, sex, or other addictions, and I break any attachments to addiction off myself. I release all trauma I have done to my life through these addictions. I nullify any words I have spoken or things that I have done to anyone who challenged my addictions. I nullify as much as I can any evil deeds or actions from any situations that arose because of those addictions. I ask mercy for all the people that I have harmed. I break these addictions off myself and I ask mercy for myself because I am the one I have harmed the most.

"I break all ties to people with whom I should never have been associated. I break all ties to people with whom I have had sex outside of marriage. I break all ties to people from whom I got a divorce or from whom I separated. I break all ties to people who try to claim some control over me, or to whom I have given control. I break off from myself the promise to keep secrets for others where that secret has brought harm into my life. I break off from myself the need to pretend someone is not a predator in my life just because they hide behind a façade. I give myself permission to recognize them for what they are and to leave the situation.

"As an act of my will, I release all feelings of being unworthy, of being abandoned, isolated, lost, left behind, discounted, or alone. I release all beliefs that I am crazy or unable to function on my own. I release any desire to hold on to these feelings.

"As an act of my will, I forgive everyone for everything. As an act of my will, I forgive myself."

REST FOR A MOMENT

As you see, that's quite a prayer. Sit for a bit and let the Holy Spirit do His work.

YOU'RE NOT DONE YET

Here's the second part of this prayer. You must do this part, too, because you need to fill the space with something of God. If you don't, one of the laws of nature is that if there is a space, it creates a vacuum. Something will come to fill it. You don't want evil coming back and filling the space because it's so nice and clean and available.

"As an act of my will, I bind to myself the love of God, the ways of God, and the thinking of God. I bind to myself His perfect love and the peace that passes understanding. I bind to myself God's perfect design for my body, his healing for my emotions and my mind. I bind to myself God's plan for my career, my relationships, my health, and my money. I bind to myself His plan for my hobbies, my weekends, my friends. I ask the Holy Spirit to fill my life and I give the Holy Spirit permission to teach me what I need to know to fix my life."

Whatever else you need, fill it in here. Don't be afraid to ask for what you need. Fill the space that has just been cleaned out in your life with all the things you most need right now to make your life better.

WHAT NOW?

I don't know what will happen for you. I can only tell you that when I did this prayer the first time, I started to feel lighter. Within a day or two I realized that I felt better. I felt at peace.

You may be thinking to yourself, "Okay, I read it, out loud, both parts, but I didn't mean it. People did things to me that really hurt and no stupid little prayer saying, 'I release it' is going to fix anything."

All I can tell you is, if you open yourself up to healing, you will be surprised. You may be surprised anyway. You have a lot of spiritual junk in your life and it doesn't matter if you can work up to any sincerity in reading those words. The main thing is to read them and let the Holy Spirit work. That's why it's an act of your will and not an act of your feelings – your feelings would prevent it, but if you choose it, then it opens up something in the spirit that changes you. It allows God to work in your life in a way that your feelings prevented before. God works with your will. You must choose. So, the prayer asks you to choose to allow God to help you. Your feelings will catch up later.

So, you think, "But how does that work? I hear you but I don't understand how what you're saying even works!" That's why I wrote the prayer out for you. You don't need to understand it, you just need to do it. Understanding will come. Right now it's about obedience. Do you want to be healed? Jesus asks this of the paralytic man in the Bible. It seems like a dumb question but there are people who don't really want to be healed. I don't think that would be you if you made it this far in this book. Choose healing. Choose life for yourself!

After I did this prayer the first time, what I found was that after a few days, more spiritual garbage started rising to the surface. Once I got rid of the initial load, then the more hidden stuff started coming up. However, it wasn't as emotionally traumatizing because I had already unloaded a boat load of junk. I started saying a variation of the prayer that was tailored just for each new particular piece of garbage that surfaced. I didn't need to sit through exhausting crying sessions with a therapist, I just needed to unload it.

Sometimes the stuff that surfaced was highly emotional, but it didn't wear me out as much to think about it and it was easier to get rid of it. I did have to face some long-hidden things. The trauma of facing something I had buried was a little difficult, but I found I could do it.

One of the main things I have experienced is a freedom from fear like I never hoped to experience. I still get afraid but I'm not paralyzed with fear anymore and I use the prayer to unload each fear that comes to me. When I start feeling afraid I pray a variation on this prayer and the fear leaves me.

DOES THIS PRAYER WORK IN A CRISIS?

I felt called to write this book. I wasn't sure I could say anything that would help people but the inspiration for this book has been filling me for awhile now. I finally chose to listen and to obey.

After I started writing, several things happened to me that have nearly knocked me flat in my life, including a major illness and attacks on my job – the greatest fears of my life all hitting me at once. As soon as I was well enough to come home from the hospital, I finally returned to this prayer and I wondered, too, if it would help me after all that had happened. But I said the prayer, tailored to all the things currently worrying me. I released the fear that the doctors had been drumming into me, I released the fear that I wouldn't heal, I released the fear that I might lose my job, I released it all. I bound to myself God's health and provision for me.

I have to say that almost immediately I started feeling better. I felt stronger. I felt like I could go on without fear. The prayer works. When the fear came back I released it again. The prayer definitely works.

In spite of what I just told you, some of you will doubtless think this prayer is too simple, that there must be more you have to do to 'earn' your freedom. Or, you find, like me, that long-buried stuff starts rising to the surface now that the first load is gone, which might make you think it didn't work. It is working. Have faith. Let go of the desire to be negative and to be proved 'right.' Embrace healing.

For those of you in desperate need of relief, now that you've been through the prayer once, I think you can be trusted to go through the journaling experience without getting so depressed that you give up before you get to the good part.

ONE LAST NOTE

One of the great kindnesses of God, one of the incredible gifts He gives us, is grace.

'Grace' is an old-fashioned word that means a special gift that is undeserved but is given anyway.

He knows we can't do this stuff on our own.

Sometimes we can't meet Him halfway. Sometimes we can barely take the first step.   Sometimes all we can do is call out.

But if we want to be rescued, God will meet us wherever we are. You can never 'earn' your way because it's impossible to be perfect, but you can ask for help and you will get it.

In the following pages, I have set up journal prompts to help you work through things a little more, if you choose. I was going to make this a journaling book and leave space to write your answers, but the first question is, how much space do I leave for each section? Some people have a lot to say, some have a little. I decided it is better to set this up a different way.

Your assignment is to go find a really nice journal, or blank book, or notebook, whatever you choose, to use in conjunction with this book. There are so many people out there making journals and blank books. The fun of finding the perfect one for you will be part of the experience.

Some of you find healing in writing. Others find healing in drawing. You can use the space to do either. Maybe drawing a picture of your feelings is more meaningful to you and more therapeutic.

Maybe you don't want to do either, maybe you prefer to leave your secrets unrevealed and would rather meditate on the questions. Or you'd rather use an iPad or a whiteboard. You can put your notes on bits of paper and tie them to tumbleweeds if you want. You have entire freedom of choice.

Now that you know how to do the prayer, as other things come to the surface, or as new events happen, you can pray some form of the prayer again to unload new spiritual junk that comes along. You need to do this prayer, or some version of it, frequently, because life is filled with spiritual junk. Don't keep the junk. Say some version of the prayer any time you're feeling like you have garbage or slime in your life.

PROMISE ME

You have to promise me one thing. Whenever you come to an issue in this book that hits you right where you live and leaves you suddenly facing old wounds, finish the exercise, however you choose to do that, and TURN THE PAGE. Don't stay stuck on that pain and reliving it. Turn the page and keep working to the solution. Because, ultimately, that's what you have to do with each of these topics, turn the page. You have carried this stuff long enough. It's time to move on. You don't need to stay stuck forever and you don't have to.

SPIRITUAL DE-CLUTTERING JOURNAL

FEAR

Fear is one of the most crippling things there is. So many of the bad things we go through have a basis of fear. I want to you to spend some time meditating on all the things of which you are afraid. In the dark of the night when no one else knows, what do you worry about? When you run into something that reminds you of things in your past, is there anything that causes you fear? When you go to the doctor, or refuse to go to the doctor, is there something of which you are afraid? Fear can be wrapped up in so many different issues. Go through what fear means to you and what you fear the most.

Once you have the initial list, I want you to construct a prayer that takes all the things of which you are most afraid, and I want you release them, piece by piece.

The next step is to construct the second half of the prayer. God tells us over and over in the Bible to have no fear. Bind to yourself God's courage, God's love, and anything else you need to help you not to be afraid anymore. Write it out and then speak it.

Let's go higher.

Were there any people who were part of your fear? People who rejected you or made fun of you or abandoned you? Someone who caused you trauma and left you with crippling fear? I want you, as an act of your will, to forgive those people. Write out all the names of anyone you thought of directly or who were implied in your fears. Doctors who gave you diagnoses, people who could have helped you and didn't. People who hurt you. All the names.

Let's go a little higher yet.

II Timothy 1:7, New King James Version

For God has not given us a spirit of fear, but of power and of love and of a sound mind.

There are several pieces to this verse. First of all, the spirit of fear doesn't come from God. So, He doesn't want you to be afraid. Power and love and a sound mind do come from God. That means that God wants you to be unafraid and he wants you to be filled with power and love. And more than that, if you are afraid you are losing your mind, God wants you to have a sound mind. You can ask for that.

What comes to you when you read these things?

POVERTY

Money. How many issues in your life revolve around issues caused by money – either too much of it or too little of it? Journal out all the good and bad things that have ever happened to you with regard to money. Start with your first experience of money and whether or not it was a positive or negative experience. Then talk about it all and say everything you need to say about money issues in your life.

All of these scenarios involve a relationship with money, good or bad. Many of them represent trauma. I want you to take everything you just wrote about, and I want you to create a prayer where you release every piece of every bad memory and every behavior that hasn't served you well.

Now I want you to bind to yourself the relationship with money that God wants you to have. And especially release the word "poor" from your vocabulary and all connection you have to poverty. Let it go. Bind to yourself God's prosperity, provision, and abundance. Write it out and then speak it.

Let's go higher.

Who has hurt you over money? They stole it, they cheated you out of it, they said nasty things, they did nasty things. You borrowed money and couldn't pay it back and the bill collectors were dreadful. You loaned money you really needed to a friend and they can't or won't pay it back. Someone embezzled money from you, someone stole your business from you, someone made you feel guilty for having money. Start writing or reflecting on who specifically has been at the root of the various money problems. And then, as an act of your will, say their names and forgive them.

John 10:10, New King James Version

The thief does not come except to steal, and to kill, and to destroy. I have come that they may have life, and that they may have it more abundantly.

There's two parts to this verse. You've been writing about times in your life when things were stolen, killed, or destroyed. Think now about what Jesus is saying here – he wants you to have life and have it abundantly. What does "abundance" mean to you? What kind of abundance could you use in your life? Ask God for it.

In the various scenarios we went through on previous pages, the reason these are so important is because the root cause of so many crimes in this world stem from people who feel something was stolen from them or that something was denied them that they were owed. Lack of money, poverty mentality, is one of the biggest sources of these angry feelings, but there are other things where you might think you were owed something that you didn't get, or that something you felt was yours was taken from you.

So many people commit crimes of all sorts because they want to avenge a theft or they want to get even with someone they think denied them something. Some of these crimes are excruciatingly violent and were committed by people who started out as sweet babies just as you did.

If you are going around filled with a kind of hate because you think you are owed something, you will accumulate all sorts of spiritual junk that will cloud your understanding very quickly. If you will let go of these feelings and let God sort it out, you can open yourself up to God's blessings. What does abundance mean to you?

If you still have feelings of anger or annoyance or rage or bitterness over financial losses, or any kind of losses, go back over the releasing prayer again and release those feelings, then bind to yourself God's peace. You need to let the junk go. It isn't serving you. Then look at the verse again. God wants to give you abundant life, but first you have to be willing to let go of all the junk and the slime that blocks it out and the negative feelings that prevent you from seeing all the places where God is already helping you. As things come to mind, release those, too, and bind to yourself God's abundance and His peace.

TRAUMA

We all have things that have traumatized us. We may not be aware of how much it hurt. Sometimes the pain is so much that we blank it out. There are all sorts of things that can cause trauma – bad childhood incidents, being a victim of crime or witnessing it, someone's suicide, someone's untimely death, a long battle with illness, murder, car accidents, betrayal, things you witnessed, war, family feuds. Start going through the things in your life that were traumatic and left scars. Maybe some of them never scarred over because they are still open wounds.

After you finish journaling, drawing, or meditating about the trauma in your life, I want you to create a prayer. It's time to let these things go. Let go of each piece of each memory.

Part of the prayer needs to be, "As an act of my will, I forgive____." And then name off all the people involved in the tragedies of your life and forgive them.

It's one of the hardest things you'll ever do but I guarantee you it will set you free.

Then I want you to bind to yourself God's healing. Let His light shine. God's light is healing. It heals wounds, it lets truth in, and the truth sets you free. Write it out and then speak it.

Let's go higher.

Deuteronomy 30:19, New Revised Standard Version

Moses has been talking to the people about all the bad things in their lives that have not served them well. And then he says to them,

19 I call heaven and earth to witness against you today that I have set before you life and death, blessings and curses. Choose life so that you and your descendants may live...."

It has always been your choice. What do you think about when you read the above?

FAMILIES

Families can be so complicated. We say things that hurt each other, we betray each other, we abandon each other, we fight for each other, we love each other, and we hate each other. Start writing about your family and all your memories and don't stop until you're finished. Go through all the family scenarios, good and bad, that explain your family and your life with them, or without them. It's time to get it all out so we can deal with it. Don't forget the family secrets.

Once you finish saying whatever you have to say, take a look at what you wrote. I bet most of the bad stuff involves fear and trauma. Before we go any farther, I want you to remember that there is nothing that has been done to you that can't be healed, and there is nothing you have done to others that can't be forgiven and healed. Nothing is so bad that God can't heal it.

I want you to construct a prayer and include each piece about your family issues that you wrote about. Write out the whole long list. A list of events and a list of the people involved.

Read it out loud and release each piece of the garbage, including any guilt you have over anything. Call back the angry words. Refuse to allow things said to you cut you anymore. Bind to yourself God's love.

Now, bind to yourself God's perfect love. Bind to yourself positive words, God's protection, God's healing, anything you need to help you cope.

Now it's time to write a prayer of forgiveness. Every bad family thing had a person behind it somewhere, even if the person was you.

You say, "But I can't forgive these people! What they did was unforgiveable!"

But you were forgiven. Every bad thing you have ever done is forgiven if you but ask.

You still think you can't do it.

Okay, so, let's look at it another way. You are so miserable, your life has been so blighted by junk from the past...WHY would you want to hang onto it any longer? Do you want to become the person who dumps all this hatred and loathing on the next generation? Or do you want to be the person who breaks these curses off your family and brings healing and hope to the next generation? Why not choose healing and hope?

Right now, it may be too much to expect you to genuinely want to forgive people. Therefore, you don't have to mean it. Just say it, out loud. Forgive everyone. Go down the list of names you produced in the things you wrote about. Say it out loud. "As an act of my will, I forgive..." and go down the list. You won't believe how much lighter you will feel. You don't need this festering mess in your life anymore. Write it out and then speak it.

Let's go higher.

Romans 8:38-39, The Voice Translation

For I have every confidence that nothing — not death, life, heavenly messengers, dark spirits, the present, the future, spiritual powers, height, depth, nor any created thing — can come between us and the love of God revealed in the Anointed, Jesus our Lord.

You are not lost and by your own choices you are being found. What does the verse above mean to you at this moment in your life?

WORDS

How many times have you had someone in your life make fun of you, or act like you were stupid, or predict that you wouldn't succeed? If you haven't had that happen then you have been blessed. For those of you who have, what was going on?

We usually call this sort of thing bullying and maybe it is. Sometimes it's a family member and the family member may not be intending to bully you, they may just be treating you like you're not right bright because...well...they're family. They might even think they are just teasing you, but you didn't take it as teasing and it hurt. But what about friends or acquaintances? Teachers? Bosses? Talk about it.

One of the hardest is the person who makes the really cutting remark and then pretends they were just kidding. This type of person is usually a friend or someone whose opinion matters to you. If it were someone we didn't care about, it wouldn't cut us. Do you know anyone who does this frequently? Do they do any other cutting things and then pretend they were 'just kidding?' Do their words just sting or do their words ever come too close to something you fear about yourself? That makes their cutting nature even harder sometimes, when we think it might be true.

How about another scenario – have you ever gotten into a nasty argument with someone and things got said to you that hurt you unbearably? Did you contribute your share by saying everything you could think of that might hurt them in return?

Has there been a time when the last thing you said to someone was the last thing they ever heard you say? Was the 'last thing' you said angry or hurtful? Some people find themselves in utter despair because they said something angry or cutting to a person and then the person died and now they can never take back what was said. They feel this will be carried into eternity and they can't forgive themselves.

First of all, if the person died, then they are in eternity and it is an earthbound belief that what you said is still harming them. If they are in heaven then nothing can hurt them ever again and if they are in hell then they have much bigger problems. Nevertheless, you can call back the words. Ask God to nullify the words you said that you wish you could take back. It is never too late.

Spend some time journaling about things that have been said to you and things you have said to others. Call back the angry words you said and release the pain of what was said to you.

Construct a prayer of forgiveness, for yourself and for others. If they have passed out of this life to the next, nullify the words and send your love to them. Whether the person is in heaven or hell is not your responsibility. You call back the words and let God sort it out.

Further than that, bind to yourself the knowledge that God created you as a special and wonderful person and that no cutting words are ever to be allowed in again. Write it out and then speak it.

Let's go higher.

Ephesians 4:26-27, The Voice Translation

[26] When you are angry, don't let it carry you into sin. Don't let the sun set with anger in your heart or [27] give the devil room to work.

Start a new life from this moment. From now on, do your best to speak life and life-giving things to people instead of angry ones. If you are longing to say, "God damn them!" about someone, change it to, "God bless them!" When you're thinking about something stupid someone did, when you mention it to someone, instead of saying, "God damn them for doing that," say, "God bless them, they sure caused a problem." Where people are being pessimistic or negative, speak hope and promise. Where people are hurling curses or gestures, speak life and hope into the situation.

Reflect on the verse above. On each piece of it. Angry, spiteful words give the devil room to work. Did you know that?

MEDICAL PROPHECIES

Medical diagnoses are some of the hardest. We tend to accept everything doctors say and not question it. If they tell us we have cancer, we ask how long we have and we go home and live with it. If they tell us that we have a serious diagnosis and that there's little hope, we believe it. If they say we must take all sorts of medicines, and then that we need more medicines to counter the medicines, we do it.

So few doctors seem to have a belief in any kind of higher power. When they have bad news to give, they really have no hope to offer because they don't believe in anything. They may even get uncomfortable with your pain and have to leave the room, or they may send an assistant with the bad news because they don't want to face you. It's almost like they failed, so they unintentionally make your health all about themselves.

I have news for you. You do not have to accept a doctor's diagnosis as final. I went with my mother and father through a lot of medical appointments. I listened to tough diagnoses and I saw how crushing it could be to the spirit if you let it. With my own recent health crisis I was given a lot of bad news and made to believe that everything was my fault and that there wasn't much hope. It's really hard not to let it crush you. I came out of the hospital filled with fear over the future. I was desperately afraid of every change in my medical condition for fear I was getting worse again. I couldn't see anything but a bleak future. I became very selfish in my thinking for awhile unintentionally because all I could see were my own problems.

I saw how the fear in certain medical diagnoses is more powerful than the disease itself. Do you have any medical conditions that scare you to death?

Let's stop right here. I don't want you to go another minute living with anything that is so frightening you can't handle it. I want you to say, out loud, with all the fierceness you can manage, "I break those words off of me. God is in charge of my times and seasons, not the doctors, not my family, not my friends, not anybody. I refuse to accept any negative prophecies over my life, including medical prophecies. I bind to myself healing and wholeness and I bind to myself courage and joy. I release all fear about my health, about my hopes, my dreams, and my future, and I bind to myself good health and good spirits so that my body and my life will come into alignment with God's plan for me."

Write about the times, any time, when someone said something to you that hurt so much you never got over it. Write about scary medical things that have happened to you.

Once you finish your journaling, do the prayer again and as you've learned, release the bad stuff and bind to yourself God's belief in you that are his beloved child and wonderfully and fearfully made. Forgive the people, including the medical people, who were involved in what you journaled about. It's time to let it all go. You've carried it long enough. Write it out and then speak it.

Let's go higher.

III John 2:2, New King James Version

Beloved, I pray that you may prosper in all things and be in health, just as your soul prospers.

What does it mean to you that you should prosper and be in health just as your soul prospers? How would spiritual and physical health be tied to your soul's health?

This book is dedicated to helping you find the balance between your soul's health, and health and prosperity for spirit, mind, and body. Here is the suggested prayer: "Lord, I release everything that might be blocking my health or the health of my soul. If there is something in my life that is blocking good health, please show me what it is and help me release it. I bind to myself your perfect healing and wholeness and your abundance and prosperity."

SPECIAL PEOPLE

My mother lost her father at a young age and she led a life that was so different from what her older brothers and sisters had experienced. After her father became very ill with tuberculosis her mother had to move the family into town from the farm and go to work to support the family. She wasn't trained for anything and so did low-skill jobs. She often worked two jobs and long hours. My mother's brothers and sisters were enough older that they had all known a relative level of stability in the family. My mother was the one who grew up in maximum uncertainty. She also became the group project for her older brothers and sisters. They said a lot of cutting things about how spoiled she was and teased her unmercifully at times. They were all athletic and thought it was hilarious that she wasn't. They tried to bully her into being more athletic. But they also loved her and they never had the slightest idea how much they hurt her.

They had all gotten to have their father's love and attention and had known many times when their mother could be available for them and could help keep the house organized and clean for them. She took them on picnics and made wonderful little parties for them. My mother was the only one who barely got to know her father before he died. Her only memories of her mother having time for her were from before the age of five. After that her mother worked many hours and things were no longer the same. My mother was the one who grew up in a world where her sisters and brothers had to do the laundry and help keep the house clean and they often refused to do it. My mother didn't want her friends to see how tousled the house was so she never invited her friends over and often spent most days after school and on weekends alone.

Her siblings all had a certain confidence born of having had a relatively stable home life. They couldn't see how she had grown up with a lot more fear than they had ever known.

Into all this loneliness and uncertainty came a grade school principal. He saw that she was left out of many things and forgotten. Somehow, in ways she never knew, she got invited to special banquets at school, or to father-daughter events put on by local civic associations, with someone designated to be her escort, and she got an award from a civic association where she never knew how she had been nominated. In later years she finally figured out that it was her principal who was quietly acting as her guardian and making sure she got included in things where otherwise, no one would have seen her or remembered her. His wife was a children's teacher who didn't particularly like children (I know, it sounds crazy but it was true), and they had no children of their own. In his own loneliness and sadness he quietly adopted my mother and watched over her. He may have watched over other forgotten children, too.

Is there anyone in your life who always goes out of their way to say kind things to you or do kind things for you, but to whom you don't pay any attention? Is there a teacher? Or a friend? Or a friend's mother or father?

There is probably someone who really tried for you but maybe you just didn't notice the way you should have. Even if you can't think of anyone, offer a prayer of gratitude right now for anyone, remembered or unremembered, who has always been there for you. Ask the Holy Spirit to reveal to you anyone who deserves your gratitude.

For those of you have remembered someone, write out what this person has done for you. And then plan something nice for that person as a way of expressing overdue gratitude. If they are already gone from this world to the next, ask Father God to do something nice for them and tell them it's from you.

Let's go higher.

There are many passages in the Bible about defending widows and orphans. Some of us have it baked into us to defend the defenseless. It's what leads so many of us to take up causes and go striding off to do battle with what we perceive to be the greatest oppressors. It is much harder, however, to look around us and find the ordinary people we meet daily who are forgotten. Look around you. Who do you pass daily somewhere in your travels who could use encouragement?

Are there elderly people whose yards need mowing or who have little handyman projects they need done? Some of them have no family to help so they must pay someone. As a result they are often cheated.

Are there children around you who never seem to be tended to by their families? Maybe you could find a non-invasive way to show care to the child.

Is there a restaurant server who seems flustered? Or a cashier who seems tired? A co-worker who seems stressed? Give them an encouraging word. You could make brownies and take them to your neighbors. There are so many things that don't cost much in time or money that you could do to help someone around you who is overlooked or forgotten.

Micah 6:8, The Voice Translation

8 No. He has told you, mortals, what is good in His sight.
   What else does the Eternal ask of you
But to live justly and to love kindness
   and to walk with your True God in all humility?

JOBS

A lot of people have an enormous amount of stress about their work. It's fulfilling, and boring, and challenging, and repetitive, and we have great bosses and terrible bosses. If you run your own business then you have all the stress of making a success out of it. You need to feed your own family and keep the business profitable so your employees can feed their families.

Start writing about your job stress, or your business stress, or meditate on it. Go through it all. The fears, the concerns, job hunting, resumes, interviews, your spouse's reactions to the issues, complications by friends and families, all of it. Don't stop until you are done – bad bosses, bad employees, lawsuits, deadlines, impossible tasks, no support, not enough resources, harassment, assault, active shooter incidents, being laid off, being fired, going bankrupt, fear you won't be able to make payroll... all of it.

I tried to write up every possible scenario you might be facing at work and there were enough to fill a book by itself. So, I just ask you to start writing and tell it your own way.

Once you get it all journaled, it's time to let the garbage go. I want you to pray the prayer of release over each piece. Then go over all the names and forgive each one as an act of your will. Say it, out loud. "As an act of my will, I forgive these people," and then name them. You don't have to mean it, that's why it's an act of your will, not of your emotions. Your emotions will catch up later. Right now you have to say it. I know they didn't ask you to forgive them but this isn't about saving them, it's about saving YOU.

Then fill this newly cleansed space with God's healing and his plan for your work life. Include wisdom, serenity, peace, anything you need. Write it out and then speak it.

Let's go higher.

Colossians 3:23-24, New Revised Standard Version

23 *Whatever task you must do, work as if your soul depends on it, as for the Lord and not for humans,* 24 *since you know that from the Lord you will receive the inheritance as your reward; you serve the Lord Christ.*

What can you do from now on to dedicate your work not to yourself or to your workplace but to God?

BETRAYAL

Many of the things we've talked about in the previous pages involve some form of betrayal. Underneath all the other issues of fear, pain, and trauma, anger, loss, and grief, there is betrayal – someone was negligent, someone didn't understand, someone didn't do their part right, someone hurt you. Someone who had the authority and the tools spent all their time on things that didn't matter and then had no energy left for the really important crisis affecting you. They did these things intentionally or unintentionally.

Go back over what you've journaled, or what you have thought about, or drawn about, and look for the moments where you were betrayed. And don't forget the places where you betrayed yourself. Write about it, and about any guilt attached to any part of these stories, because guilt is part of self-betrayal.

Maybe they didn't mean to hurt you, maybe they did. Maybe you didn't mean to screw up but it happened. Or maybe you went totally crazy and chose to do something only to realize later what a mess you had made of everything. Maybe you were in such despair that you thought, "Screw it, nothing matters anyway so why not?" And then later when you started caring again you saw what you had done to yourself.

Sometimes the end result involves depression. One good thing I got out of seeing counselors was something one of them said to me – "Depression is a silent temper tantrum. Who are you so angry with you are turning it in on yourself?" It was an excellent question. If you are struggling with depression, ask yourself this question: Who are you angry with?

Make a list. Write or speak this list just between you and God. Lay out every situation, every person involved where you feel a wrong was done to you. Don't leave anything behind.

Do this alone, in your room, behind closed doors. Talk to God. If you're angry with God, tell Him about it. Yell at Him if you need to, He can take it. It's okay to be hurt and angry. It's okay to be frustrated, or grieving. Then forgive that person. Forgive God if you have to. Forgive yourself.

The only way you will ever get better is to get the poison out of your system and then heal the system. If you insist on hanging onto your grievances, you will never get the poison out and you will never get healed.

Even if you are convinced you are right, even if you know the person will never ask your forgiveness in return, forgive them anyway. Right now we're working on freeing YOU. It's important to get the spiritual junk out of you and get rid of it in such a way that it doesn't come back. And we don't want to leave spiritual junk lying around for someone else to get tangled up with. Neutralizing it is the only way, and the only way to neutralize it is to take away its power to hurt you.

You know what's coming, but you can do this.

After you go through everything and everyone that has really hurt you, I want you to go through again and forgive each person involved.

This is between you and God and no one else. This is not the time to lie to yourself or to shade the truth. It's not the time to minimize what you did or what someone else did to you, or to try to pretend it wasn't as bad as it really was. Lay it all out. Release it and let it go. Write it out and then speak it.

Now you need to go through each thing where you blame yourself and you need to forgive yourself.

Some of you have carried things with you for years and no matter what anyone says, you've been totally unable to let it go. You've blamed yourself and agonized over it in the dark of the night for a long time. You might even have nightmares about it or be unable to sleep. The noise in your head is so loud it drowns out everything else.

What do you do?

Well, you say, out loud, "As an act of my will, I forgive myself." And you go over each item you listed.

Your Father loves you so much he cries with you. He does not want you tied up your whole life, unable to function. Imagine yourself sitting with your Father, someone who loves you so much He knows every tiny detail about you. He knows you and He loves you anyway. Speak to Him as though He's next to you. Say all the things you've been journaling about.

WHAT IF...WHAT IF YOU MISUNDERSTOOD?

It's entirely possible that some of the things you've been journaling about are things that you totally misunderstood. Maybe you were offended over something that was never ever meant in an offensive way. Maybe you weren't allowing for your parents to be humans who make mistakes. Maybe even the worst things they did, you can, in fact, understand because as an adult you've been in equally difficult circumstances. And yet you hung onto your childhood grievances.

I thought about that when I was writing this book, that maybe we are accepting a grievance as legitimate that has no basis in reality. But I came to the conclusion that if you think the offense was real then we have to treat it as real because you are carrying it around with you and it's holding you back. Now that you have shed a few tons of spiritual junk, ask the Holy Spirit to work in you and teach you. Ask about these situations, to show you what was really going on.

For some of these situations, maybe they really were as bad as you thought. Maybe they were even worse. Maybe you really were to blame. Maybe you weren't. Maybe there was a predator in your life who made sure to set you up to blame yourself for everything the predator was doing to you. Continuing to blame yourself for things where there was an elaborate trap laid for you is counter-productive.

How can you know the difference? How can you know if you were to blame, or not to blame, or if you misunderstood? Until you started shedding the junk, there was no room to sort out anything. Now you can. Places where you could let it go because it wasn't as big as you thought. Places you need to forgive yourself. Places where you need to know you got tangled up with an evil person and you can't take on their junk as your own.

PREDATORS

Years ago I was working with a person who functions as a counselor. She helped me a lot with some things and she worked with me from a mental health standpoint. I did all the things she counseled me to do and it did work. I was losing weight, I was getting more confident, I was happier. She was a professing Christian but she didn't seem to have much of a view of God except from a distance. She was more concerned about informing me that telling bawdy jokes and cussing and living like a non-Christian was permissible. In her view, Christians weren't bound anymore by the 'old rules.' And I let her tell me all that and I believed her. I was impressed with her 'freedom' from what the neighbors might think and I strove to be like her. I, too, started shedding concerns about the 'old morality.'

After I got out of her course, I was doing so well. But it was almost immediately after I finished her course that I met up with someone who was the biggest predator I've ever met. And I was completely ripe to be taken over by him. I had no shields, I had no power in my faith, I had no understanding of how evil he really was. He got me to betray myself and then laughed about it gleefully. He got me to make decisions that wrecked my life. My family was totally opposed and I was so hooked by him that I chose him over my family, causing a rift that took years to heal.

He started by separating me from my friends. And then my family. And pretty soon my job came under fire. I didn't see what was happening to me until the day came when, after all his coaching on how to get through job interviews, I finally landed a good job. We'd been working on it for weeks. However, when I told him, he was livid. He berated me and told me how stupid I was and how the minute he could he was going to get me fired. I had barely started and he was already jealous of my boss. I was so lost. Wasn't this what we had worked for all these months? Wasn't this the future we had discussed? It took a long time for me to grasp that he didn't really want me to do anything that would give me confidence or help me feel independent. He wanted me totally dependent on him. The day he went off on me about my success he killed something in me. It was the beginning of me seeing the terrible trap I had stepped into thinking I was getting free.

But before all that I got pregnant. And I had just learned he was in trouble with the law and probably headed to prison. I was beyond frightened. How was I going to care for this baby by myself and as the wife of a convict? How had I fallen so far down that I was living a hedonistic life with a person in trouble with the law to the point where I got pregnant with his child? And then I began learning what types of things he had really been involved in and I got really scared. How could I bring this child into the world with this kind of father? But even before learning about what he had really been involved in, I was desperate to fix the situation so I made him marry me.

The first thing that happened after I got pregnant was Valentine's Day. And what did he do? He decided that there was some girl at work who understood him better so he actually gave her more of a present than he gave me. I was pregnant with his child but this chick at work meant the same or more to him than I did. And then he decided that he didn't need to be home with me so much as he needed to go party. One memorable night he didn't come home and he didn't call. I flipped out worrying about him and he was furious with me later about it. Anytime I tried to surprise him with a nice meal or a special day he would manage to start an argument and ruin it.

I eventually realized somewhere deep down that he was a predator. I wouldn't admit it to myself but I was desperately afraid of bringing a child into the world with him as the father. I got an abortion. What I didn't know was that I would never get another chance to be with someone and have a baby. I never should have gotten the abortion but also I never should have been having sex with him in the first place. One mistake brought on many other mistakes and they all brought on lies and bad choices and disaster. I never told people I had gotten an abortion, I told them I had miscarried. I lied to people for years about him and about the baby and about everything that had happened. And I blamed myself for all of it because I thought I had made a choice. I had, but the choices were all based on lies. He was a predator. He somehow knew everything to say to me and just exactly the way to say it to get me hooked and keep me hooked until it was too late.

It took me years to understand how I could have been so stupid. I can't explain the whole episode with him without revealing an incredible level of stupidity on my part.

And then I found this verse in the Bible.

Matthew 12:43-45, New King James Version

43 *When an unclean spirit goes out of a man, he goes through dry places, seeking rest, and finds none. 44 Then he says, 'I will return to my house from which I came.' And when he comes, he finds it empty, swept, and put in order. 45 Then he goes and takes with him seven other spirits more wicked than himself, and they enter and dwell there; and the last state of that man is worse than the first. So shall it also be with this wicked generation.*

I never understood that passage before but I think the Holy Spirit steered me there because it directly applied to my life. I suddenly saw my life in a new perspective. This counselor and I had cleaned out my life by concentrating on my mental health, but we didn't replace it with anything of God and we never addressed the spiritual issues. In fact, her view of God seemed to be that Christians were old fuddy-duddies and that being able to cuss and swear and have sex when you wanted to was all to the good. So, we had tidied up my mental health and I was all cleaned out and set up. And at that precise moment, in walked an incredibly evil predator type person and just took me over. He knew all the things to say to make me think he cared about me and he was very convincing.

After I was good and hooked he changed his approach. Suddenly I wasn't cherished anymore. He started treating me more and more like a piece of trash. We had an argument one time and he informed me that he owned me. He got in my face with the angriest eyes I've ever seen and told me I had no right to do anything that upset him because he owned me. After I met him some of the most devastating things I ever went through happened to me. It took years to recover.

This is why it's so important to do both parts of the prayer. You need to clear out the junk and you need to fill the space with God so that nothing else can move in that's worse than where you started. In time, if you ask, the Holy Spirit will help you sort out what you did, and what was done to you. What of your experiences you totally own and what you don't own. Right now, you need to get rid of the junk so that your mind is clear enough to understand what you need to understand.

Go back over any items you've been journaling and say the prayers again if you need to. And say again that you forgive people. If you remain filled with hate and anger and unforgiveness, you can be controlled through those emotions and persuaded to do things you shouldn't do, or, be taken over by impulses that lead you to do things you really shouldn't do. If you neutralize it, then evil can't control you because there's nothing to control. If you use God's power to forgive, it's over. You can't be taken over through those emotions if you get rid of them. You will have peace. Write it out and then speak it.

Pray the prayer every time the feelings come up. Jesus told us to forgive as many times as its needed. Do it. Stop fighting it and just do it. It sets you free.

Shattered Soul

When I got free from the predator, when I started recovering from all the terrible things that had gone wrong in my life while I was with him, I came to a point of utter desolation. I felt as though my soul had been shattered into a thousand fragments. I had made some terrible decisions and after I left him I sought comfort from people who hurt me almost as bad as he had. Sometimes they hurt me unintentionally but they still hurt me. Every new betrayal broke off another little piece of me and scattered it somewhere. Every person I developed a tie to took a piece of me away with them and I felt like I would never find all the pieces of myself.

And then one day I heard this Psalm with new ears, new understanding:

Psalm 23:1-3, New King James Version

A Psalm of David.

23 The Lord is my shepherd;

> *I shall not want.*

2 He makes me to lie down in green pastures;

> *He leads me beside the still waters.*

3 He restores my soul;

> *He leads me in the paths of righteousness*

> *For His name's sake.*

Look at verse 3. "*He restores my soul.*" I have heard this Psalm my whole life and I never looked at that sentence before. He restores my soul. That means God WANTS to restore my soul and CAN restore my soul. If you are like me and have been through terrible things, you may feel, as I did, that your soul is fragmented, like you are scattered everywhere. You may feel that it is beyond being restored, that it can't all be put back together. But if God knows how many hairs are on your head (Matthew 10:30, *But the very hairs of your head are all numbered*) then He knows where every piece of you is. If He knows where it is, then He would help you put it all back together.

When you read this, how do you feel? What do you think about?

Write a prayer and ask the Lord to restore you. Ask Him to put back together all the scattered bits. With the work you've been doing in reading this book, you have done the preliminary work to remove all the blockages on your side that would prevent you being restored. Ask.

DREAMS

Now that you have begun to emerge from under that pile of junk, things you used to dream about may start returning to you.

There's another round of releasing and binding to do. Maybe someone laughed you out of your dreams or bad things happened and you gave up. What has held you back? I want you to journal it. What did you use to dream you wanted to be or do? And then what stopped you?

It's time to construct a prayer. Create a prayer where you release all your doubts and fears about following your dreams. Name all the things you wish you could change about your life. Add in all the things you discussed above. The problems may go back to the previous stuff you journaled – old traumas, people who made fun of you, crippling fear, anything like that. Then, as an act of your will, release them. Bind to yourself God's confidence, energy, and talent. His plans, His ways, His visions, His dreams. Write it out and then speak it.

Let's go a little higher.

If you are really serious about wanting to rebuild your life into something better, ask God to clear away all the obstacles in your path and show you where to start. Better yet, ask God to give you HIS dreams for your life. He has much better ideas than you do, anyway. Ask Him for the help you need to get started. Are you willing to let God guide you?

RINSE AND REPEAT

It's time to go over the prayer again. It's time to cover the ground again now that you have a more educated perspective and we've cleared away the first load. Let's go for the best you we can get. Let's not assume that you're beyond repair. I don't care what it looks like in this world, God can do anything.

THE PRAYER

"As an act of my will, I lay all the things I have been journaling about before Jesus and I release them. I release all the negative feelings, the terrible memories, the failures, the losses, the moments when I have felt betrayed, the moments I betrayed myself, the causes I have been consumed by, the stresses from my work, the bad choices, the addictions, all of it. I release it all.

"As an act of my will, I forgive everyone for everything. As an act of my will, I forgive myself.

"As an act of my will, I leave vengeance to God and I will devote myself to Godly justice. I bind to myself God's perspective and God's ways.

"As an act of my will, I bind to myself the love of God, the ways of God, and the thinking of God. I bind to myself His perfect love and the peace that passes understanding. I bind to myself God's perfect design for my body, his healing for my emotions and my mind. I bind to myself God's plan for my career, my relationships, my health, and my money. I bind to myself His plan for my hobbies, my weekends, my friends. I ask the Holy Spirit to fill my life. I give the Holy Spirit permission to teach me what I need to know to fix my life."

MY FINAL BLESSING TO YOU

I want you to be free, with true freedom. I call forth blessings for you, of peace and prosperity, of provision and abundance. And I call forth the ways of God to fill your life. And joy. I call forth joy for you.

The words of Jesus for you:

John 14:27, New King James Version

27 Peace I leave with you, My peace I give to you; not as the world gives do I give to you. Let not your heart be troubled, neither let it be afraid.

.